Hanna's Big Adventure.
Copyright © 2021 Evelyn Audet
Produced and printed
by Stillwater River Publications.
All rights reserved. Written and produced in the
United States of America. This book may not be reproduced
or sold in any form without the expressed, written
permission of the author and publisher.
Visit our website at
www.StillwaterPress.com
for more information.
First Stillwater River Publications Edition
Library of Congress Control Number: 2021900930
Paperback ISBN: 978-1-952521-80-5
1 2 3 4 5 6 7 8 9 10
Written by Evelyn Audet.
Illustrated by Lia Marcoux.
Published by Stillwater River Publications,
Pawtucket, RI, USA.
Publisher's Cataloging-In-Publication Data
(Prepared by The Donohue Group, Inc.)

Names: Audet, Evelyn, author. | Marcoux, Lia, illustrator.
Title: Hanna's big adventure / written by Evelyn Audet ; illustrated by Lia Marcoux.
Description: First Stillwater River Publications edition. | Pawtucket, RI, USA : Stillwater River Publications, [2021] | Interest age level: 005-009. | Summary: "Rescued from a local pound, Hanna joins her new family and sails aboard a luxurious yacht in the Caribbean. Throughout her adventure, she teaches her new family about love and exuberance for life as she becomes part of her new family and crew"--Provided by publisher.
Identifiers: ISBN 9781952521805 (paperback)
Subjects: LCSH: Dog rescue--Juvenile fiction. | Dog owners--Family relationships--Juvenile fiction. | Human-animal relationships--Juvenile fiction. | Sailing--Caribbean Sea--Juvenile fiction. | CYAC: Dog rescue--Fiction. | Dog owners--Family relationships--Fiction. | Human-animal relationships--Fiction. | Sailing--Caribbean Sea--Fiction. | LCGFT: Action and adventure fiction.
Classification: LCC PZ7.1.A94 Ha 2021 | DDC [E]--dc23

The views and opinions expressed in this book
are solely those of the author
and do not necessarily reflect the
views and opinions of the publisher.

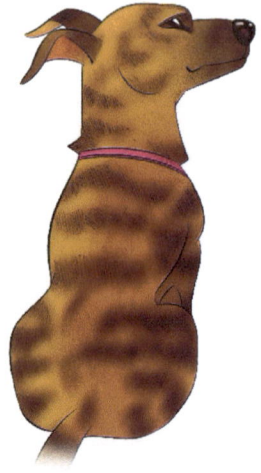

Hanna waited by the door for her owner. She needed to pee and was hungry. But no one came. Day after day, no food, no humans, no going outside, and no clean water.

After a long week, the dogcatcher broke open the door.
He forced Hanna into a van and then into a cage.

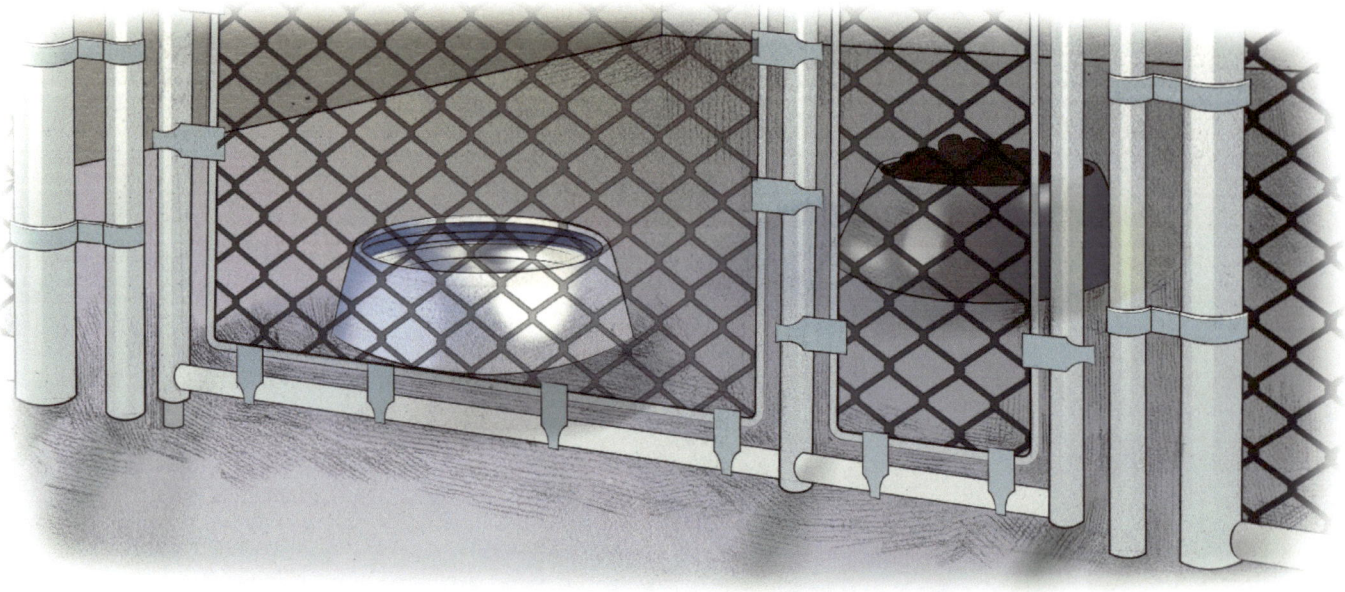

Hanna felt as if she was in jail and wanted to be outdoors. So she broke the latch to get into the outer cage where she would spend the next four miserable weeks.

Then one brutally cold day, Hanna watched intently as a couple came into the parking lot. After much ballyhoo, the couple put a leash on her, put her in a truck, and brought her to a house.

The couple, Mom and Steve, welcomed Hanna into their lives. Their home was warm and kind, with comfortable beds for rest, great food, and lots of toys. They had several cars and trucks, and two buildings with plenty of places to play. The mom even called her truck, "Hanna's Truck" because Hanna liked it so much.

After two joyful years, on a chilly wintery day, Hanna was put into her crate in the back of Hanna's Truck. She was being taken away from her home. She was afraid that Mom and Steve were taking her back to that jail.

Instead, the crate was locked inside the belly of a big airplane! Hanna was cold, alone, and frightened.

She flew for what seemed like an eternity in the rattling darkness. Hanna had to pee and was very hungry.

When the airplane bumped to a skidding stop, Hanna discovered it was hot outside. There were new smells and strange trees that looked like umbrellas.

She happily wagged herself into circles when she saw Mom and Steve!

Steve built a funny contraption so Hanna could climb in and out of her new home, high off the ground. They called the home a sailboat. Hanna thought of it as "Hanna's Boat".

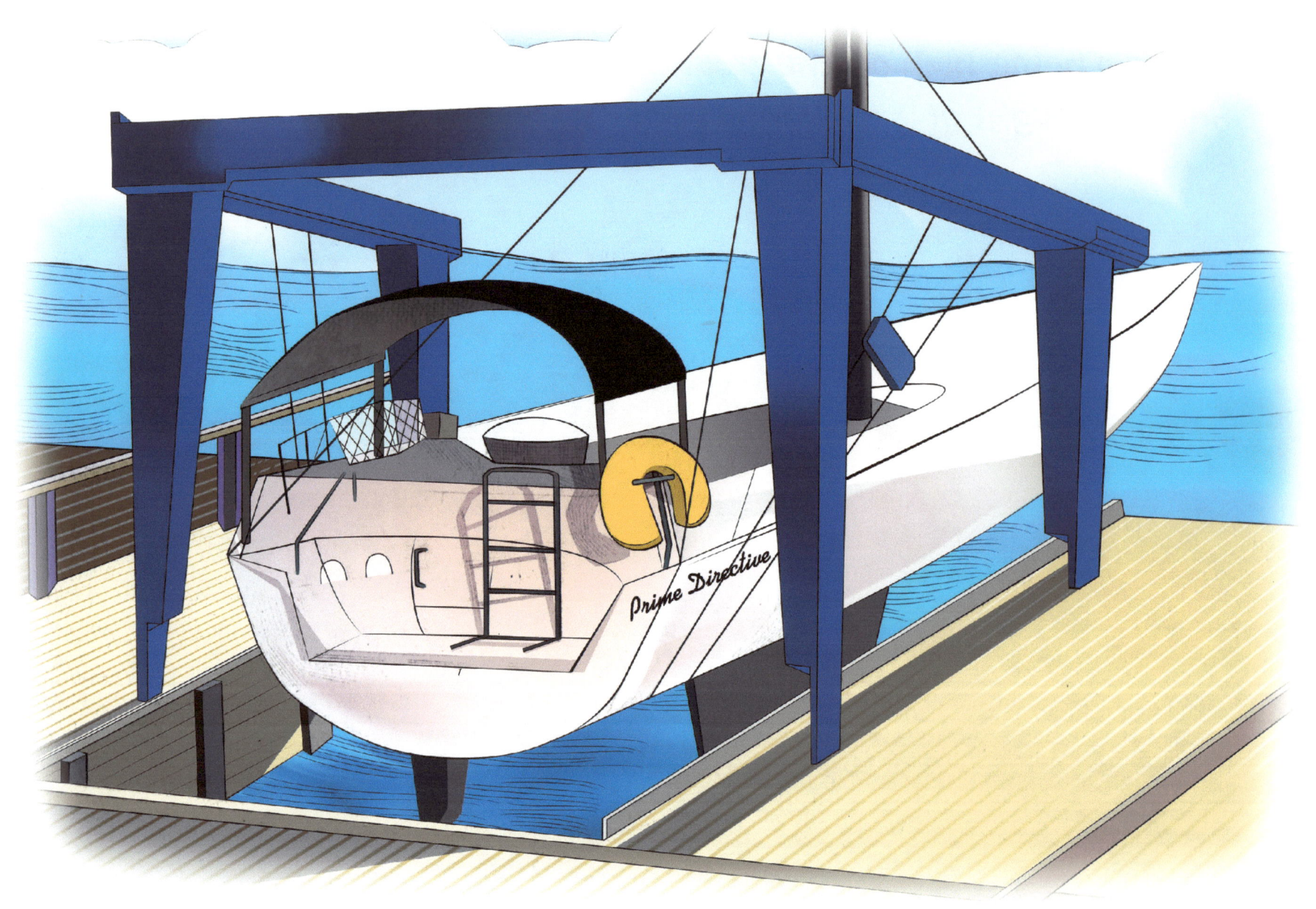

A big crane lowered Hanna's Boat into the water.

Mom and Steve got a little boat called a dinghy for quick rides on the sea.

Hanna proudly became the bowsprit, so Mom named it "Hanna's Dinghy".

When Captain Steve said, "Coming About!" Hanna learned to move from one side of the sailboat to the other.

Hanna learned that ropes on a boat are called lines and she learned how to keep watch.

Hanna became an important part of the crew.

Several times a day, Captain Steve took Hanna to shore.

She manned the bow of the dinghy, frolicked on the shore, sniffed scents, and did her business.

Some days, she stayed at anchor.
Hanna liked to watch the kids play in the cove

... and then she would take a nap.

Other days, she went on a safari bus ride or hung out with friends.
Some days, she would ride with friends on fast powerboats.

And on other days, she went to a nearby park to sit under the palm trees

or to visit the beach for some island time.

On the greatest days, Hanna played in the water.

She learned to swim like a fish.

When Captain Mom launched the floating mats,
it added a whole new challenge for Hanna.

Hanna wriggled and jiggled the mat until her toy fell off.

Then she swam to fetch it from the water.

Then she climbed back onto the mat to do it all over again.

Hanna enjoyed swimming but soon learned...

...that jumping was the best!

Hanna taught herself to climb the swim ladder so she could swim, climb and...

...JUMP! And JUMP! And JUMP!

Captain Steve would say, "OK, That's enough!"
Then she spent tranquil time on her floating home.

She ate delicious food
and Hanna was content to be with her loving family.

And finally, at the end of each enchanting day,
Hanna slept outside under the stars with Captain Mom.

About the Author

Captain Evelyn Audet has a tale to tell. This is her first book in a progression of three, each expanding in detail for maturing audiences. The family of three, the third being the dog, traveled to their sailboat to escape Rhode Island winters sailing the United States and British Virgin Islands. Every day brought a new adventure. Evelyn grew up in Westport, Massachusetts and lives in Rhode Island with Captain Steve and they enjoy their journey of life. We love you our dear pet, Hanna. You were such an important part of our lives for the short 11 years 8 months and 5 days we had the pleasure of sharing life with you.

About the Illustrator

Lia Marcoux is a 2009 Rhode Island School of Design graduate in Illustration. Working as an illustrator, she is currently based in Somerville, Massachusetts. Her work is a blend of watercolor and digital media, with a focus on clear line and vibrant color. A native New Englander, she has yet to visit the Caribbean, but it's definitely on her to-do list!

www.ingramcontent.com/pod-product-compliance
Lightning Source LLC
LaVergne TN
LVHW072356110526
838202LV00103B/2621